POEMS
NEW & SELECTED

Patrick Lane

TORONTO
Oxford University Press
1978

Canadian Cataloguing in Publication Data

Lane, Patrick, 1939–
    Poems, new and selected

ISBN 0-19-540296-0 pa.

I. Title.

PS8523.A5A17 1978   C811'.5'4   C78-001559-2
PR9199.3.L352A17 1978

THIS BOOK IS FOR MY SONS MICHAEL AND RICHARD

Some of these poems were first published in *NMFG,
Canadian Literature, Event, The Malahat Review, The
Tamarack Review, Toronto Life*, and by Harbour
Publishing. Grateful acknowledgement is made to the
House of Anansi for permission to include poems from
Beware the Months of Fire.

Other books by Patrick Lane

LETTERS FROM THE SAVAGE MIND

SEPARATIONS

ON THE STREET

MOUNTAIN OYSTERS

HIWAY 401 RHAPSODY

THE SUN HAS BEGUN TO EAT THE MOUNTAIN

PASSING INTO STORM

BEWARE THE MONTHS OF FIRE

UNBORN THINGS

ALBINO PHEASANTS

Cover painting by Robert Daigneault
Publication of this book was assisted by the Canada Council
© Patrick Lane
ISBN 0-19-540296-0
1 2 3 4 — 1 0 9 8
Printed in Canada by Webcom Limited

Contents

CONTENTS

CONTENTS

THE BEE-CAVE

Sitting in the bee-cave
beneath Okanagan hills
I look out to yellow

of mountain sunflowers
and wrap my closed breath
around the droning

of bees that in
the darkness nest

I bare my belly
to their smooth stings
and measure swelling

by years they are
away on desolate trips
Sing bees of the lonely caves

why do you travel
back into this darkness?

PROSPECTOR

Old man you prospected summer
country of caves and gold.
With the rattlesnake and spider
you were a black widow without a mate
gone deep chrome yellow.
You shared with the sun
a babble of flowers and full
brown flawless centers where
you walked in a wilderness
of golden sleep.

Once I was a child
and saw you touch a mountain
wasp with your finger
tip to wing he didn't move
but shivered gently his petal shells
of yellow and black in the wide corner
of August. You watched solitary
wasps float down sunflower fields.

Old man I dreamed you
wandered the mountains
in spring and planted
the hills with golden flowers.
When they found you
they said you were dead
but I knew that the wasps
had planted their eggs in you
and flowers were growing
out of your sleeping eyes.

NEWSPAPER WALLS

And the newspaper walls to keep the heat in.
A diary of packed-in dreams
overland from Kamloops
to a land-locked lake.

   Who split the cedar,
   took beaver poplar
   for table-legs and shelves,
   carved the sash
   at home
   on the North Thompson—
   broken windows and mouse seed?

Thirty-one days of August
1915
stare out at a room—
no sheet crumbled, burned
to find September's turn.

   Where was home then—
   after the deluge?

LOVING SHE STOOD APART

loving she stood apart
and looked at me wanting
her and afraid she was
of the wanting to need
me watching her from
where I lay on the bed
as she undressed

and turned her back
to me undressed her
back was smooth the
angle of her hip so
I could touch her
holding my hand beside me
feet from where she was
her hands soft fingers
reaching out to me
from where they rested
on her shoulders afraid
to turn around and see me
see her eyes

turn out the light

she said and when I
made no move to move
my eyes to blackness
and the loss she said

please . . .

so quietly my mind
shut out the sight
and I was blind to
her but O the night

CALGARY CITY JAIL

Today they took him away
and lonely in my cell I read the walls—
the names the thousand jagged scrawls
in slivers of words
in languages I don't know.

And I think, he's gone
and what the hell?

Yesterday he spent the hours
capturing roaches
in his cramped rachitic hand
and after supper
took a dented can
and smashed them all.

He laughed when I carved my name above my bed.
What does it matter? he said
they'll only paint you over.

CARIBOO WINTER

Snow has burned the rocks

    the ground is cold

and a whimpering wind
has curled the empty
fields with sheets of ice

      in my gloves
      my fingers
      grasp at nothing
      . . . turn and turn again

Silent trees are airborn
and hills a shifting
mist in the pallid sky

      my flesh recoils

soon it will snow again

TEN MILES IN FROM HORSEFLY

Ten miles in from Horsefly
shoulders sore from my pack
feet blistered I asked for
and got a job cleaning a barn
for the price of a meal
and the promise I could sleep
outside the unseasonal rain
and worked like a damn
as digger flies took chunks
of meat from my arms
and mosquitoes sucked my blood.

No one knows how far an hour goes
or how short are the days.
Shovelling ten months of shit
from a barn clears your head
and allows you to look forward
to sleep without fear or favour
from old sad dreams of enemies
and friends. Just to have one moment
with shoulders clear of weight
and feet braced finally still
as you come breathless
to the clear hard boards below.

BECAUSE I NEVER LEARNED

For John

Because I never learned how
to be gentle and the country
I lived in was hard with dead
animals and men I didn't question
my father when he told me
to step on the kitten's head
after the bus had run over
its hind quarters.

Now, twenty years later,
I remember only:
the silence of the dying
when the fragile skull collapsed
under my hard bare heel,
the curved tongue in the dust
that would never cry again
and the small of my father's back
as he walked tall away.

ELEPHANTS

The cracked cedar bunkhouse
hangs behind me like a grey pueblo
in the sundown where I sit
to carve an elephant
from a hunk of brown soap
for the Indian boy who lives
in the village a mile back
in the bush.

The alcoholic truck-driver
and the cat-skinner sit beside me
with their eyes closed
all of us waiting out the last hour
until we go back on the grade

and I try to forget the forever
clank   clank   clank
across the grade
pounding stones and earth to powder
for hours in mosquito darkness
of the endless cold mountain night.

The elephant takes form—
my knife caresses smooth soap
scaling off curls of brown
which the boy saves to take home
to his mother in the village

Finished, I hand the carving to him
and he looks at the image of the great
beast for a long time
then sets it on dry cedar
and looks up at me:
                    What's an elephant?
he asks
so I tell him of the elephants
and their jungles. The story
of the elephant graveyard
which no one has ever found
and how the silent
animals of the rain forest
go away to die somewhere
in the limberlost of distances
and he smiles

tells me of his father's
graveyard where his people have been
buried for years. So far back
no one remembers when it started
and I ask him where the graveyard is
and he tells me it is gone
now where no one will ever find it
buried under the grade of the new
highway.

WILD HORSES

Just to come once alone
to these wild horses
driving out of the high Rockies
raw legs heaving the hip-high snow.
Just once alone. Never to see
the men and their trucks.

Just once alone. Nothing moves
as the stallion with five free mares
rush into the guns. All dead.
Their eyes glaze with frost.
Ice bleeds in their nostrils
as the cable hauls them in.

Later, after the swearing
and the stamping of feet
we ride down into Golden:

Quit bitchin.
It's a hard bloody life
and a long week
for three hundred bucks of meat.

That and the dull dead eyes
and the empty meadows.

SIMILKAMEEN DEER

Driving through the Similkameen valley
I watch for deer on the road.
Miles roll out beneath me. A telegraph key.
A perpetual line of dots.
                              Men here
have put up signs telling me to watch
for rolling rock under the escarpment
of mountains where they've cut stones
for their convenience.

Soon it will be spring and mountains
will lose their somnolence. Snow will melt
and out of a fading
whiteness of mountain cold
there will be deer somewhere
who will have no time to spend
watching for me.

JULIE

Moving through grass country
on the flat land by the river
I watch the buckboard roll
slowly, tied together with baling
wire and rust where men stand
throwing spruce boughs beneath
wheels to move it through
the deep places and I want
to do something more than stand
here stripping branches from the trees.

One night I knelt by her crib
and listened to her hunger shriek
while trees tossed softly
in the wind. I can't forget
the years I want to damn.

Julie is dead in Kamloops
by the long blue river
and the morning is full of loons.

FOR TEN YEARS

Tonight the moon slants cold into the snow.
Ice shudders on the glass and suddenly alone
I'm aware of windows. Was it you who told me
you were gone? Beyond the snow
light rides thin as a broken bow
without a hand to guide it. From this hour
darkness comes shrill as a dying bird.

One night in the north you lay in my arms
and wept for a crying bird. In the morning
you found him dead on the window-sill.
His beak was a crust of ice
that melted as you breathed.
When I threw him away, he didn't fly.
That country of snow we lived in
was a cushion for owls to walk on.
Birds don't understand windows.
They never did.

LAST NIGHT IN DARKNESS

Last night in darkness someone killed our cat.
Dipped her in gas. Set her aflame.
Her scattered kittens adorned the yard
in opaque sacks where she aborted them
none of them burned in her pain.

As I gathered them in a paper bag
I had to pull off slugs
who'd gathered for the feast.
Their scavenger trails hovered
on her body like a mist.

Just to forget her
I leaned heavy in the morning
thrusting with my shovel
deep into earth behind the daisies
reminded only of the other
graves I'd dug

while my son prepared them
for peace, took each one
out of their paper coffin,
drove apple blossoms into their eyes -
even the mother who was so scarred.

THERE WAS A WOMAN BENDING

There was a woman bending
her body on a bed
curved like a statue carved from life.
In her hand was a twisted thing
black as the hair
that hung like a broken wing.
She lived down the hall from me.

Everything about her smelled of death.
I want to tell you of the foetus
speared on a knitting needle
and blood thick as grease
between her thighs.

There was this woman I saw once on a bed
her body curved like a statue, dead.
I've forgotten her name.
It was the walls her eyelids made
that I remember. The silences they bred.

And her eyes,
eyes I will never know the colours of.

SASKATCHEWAN

Covering my shaking
I roll this cigarette
hard in the wind.

I left so much in you:
your belly will always hold
the curves I made. You danced
for me, swollen with the second child.
That was eight years ago and now
I can't find you anywhere —
only this flat prairie
and an unhealed bruise
of cloud that won't go down.
As the land retreats
there's nothing to touch,
nothing to hold onto.

Only this shaking
and this last match
I'm afraid to light
in the wind
in the empty land.

TESTAMENTS

The grass you crushed as you rolled away
has brushed the leaves between us
into a bed of broken stems.
Don't ask again.
When I hurt you it wasn't anger.
You want to know my dreams.
You want too much.

In my dreams I see
the men and graven women
huddle beside the stacks
of starving children at Dachau.
Come away from the fence.
In the distance between us
you're like a body left behind
at Treblinka. We must make love again.

I promise you I won't sleep.
I won't look at the sun.
Keep me awake and my eyes,
born to a futile anger, will relearn
their gentleness.
                    Awake I keep alive
the mockery our fathers left us; asleep
they lie with me in a common grave.

FOR RITA — IN ASYLUM

In candle-spiked darkness of the coffee-house
I watched tonight your last
your temporary lover
who remembered you for me
over a cup of espresso
and the laughter of his friends.
He was happy.
Two weeks had gone by
and he still wasn't diseased.

Now I walk between two tenements
where grass grows yellow
and in the wind
bends like strange weeping
hair on your thin white face.
Rita you said
only a fool walks in a singing rain
but tonight I'm sick and the rain
no longer sings.
Cars pass me in the night.
Their tires crease hard wet streets
and water folds back on their passing.

Tonight you sleep in asylum
where no man can give you grace.
Across the street
is the hollow of stone
that was a marketplace for your womb.
Like a woman you said
that building is full of holes.

SURCEASE

Here in this car is surcease from a thousand dead,
a woman and a bottle and the rain.

Used car chrome crumbles into dust
and broken windows stain with smears of rust,
each rock-scarred shivered pane
creased with a crust of red. Your eyes
in darkness will never see why you're afraid
and why I'm drunk.

Only hours can drain away the sudden
years, pits I've placed my dead in.
I don't want words from you.

Tonight I want to turn with you to neon
blue as the stiff veins under your tongue
and don't say: Give it time
say nothing
to hell with time.
Take off your clothes. Hang
your breasts in my eyes. I want
to ride with your body and celebrate
the darkness and my pain . . .
forget the past.

Play with me gently, woman,
I'm made of glass.

MY FATHER'S FACE

My father's face
with sunshine cracked and razed
hangs above
a fallen twisted pine
he carried
down from the distant hills

Under the sun
the silences lie dazed

A grass stem falls
a brittle stone is crazed
where earth absorbs
the harsh caress of heat

and my father
with his axe riding the sky
opens wounds
and pinewood falls away
in mounds of bleeding
yellow at my feet
where the scent of pitch
mixes with the sun

LOADING BOXCARS

Drawn by spilled grain
and terrified by the switch-engine
the blue-jay has broken its fingernail skull
on the wall of the boxcar.

Bird's claws attach to nothing
clench on cold air. Wild voices
are stilled only by eating and death.
I am afraid of what I don't know.
Parasite flies crawl hopeless among feathers.
Soon they will leave
in search of a living bird.

Blue wings harden in my hand.
Bones crack, hollow as wind
where it creeps on high snow
levelling mountains with the land.

HASTINGS STREET ROOMS

A wall is two sides. Here
on the inside there is nothing
to hang and I sit looking
at bare spaces around me.

On the outside is another
man. He has painted his walls
in many colours, hung pictures
of his loved ones.
Their screams come through
the plaster like shredded fingers.

A wall is two sides.
I would cut a window
but all that I would add
would be four more walls
and silence
like a painting of tomorrow.

THAT THERE SHOULD BE NO SECRET

I have handled your body like a crayon.
Colours of you are smeared on my legs,
oily sweat
and a hard circle of blood.
Inside you is a bleeding.
The bite a shark leaves, clean,
taken in leisure. I am proud
and angry at your loss —
this ritual plundering.
What can I say?

You look at me now,
your eyes delicate as a fish
dancing in water and you laugh,
take back what I have taken
and hold it to you
like an old doll found in a box.

GRAY SILK TWISTING

I stick my tongue in you,
move like a great fluid worm
eating out your soul. At night
I was told our souls leave our bodies
through our mouths
but I know it leaves every hole
like gray silk twisting,
tasting of earth.

I enter you this way,
my eyes in your hair,
my fingers gripping the smooth
lips of you. Without speaking
you wrap your gray inside me
as I dance
finally thigh to thigh
attached to you by hooks,
tearing me as I come.

POEM FOR A GONE WOMAN

I breathe in the mouth
of a blue snake
who lies broken in the mountains.
In his mouth a frog struggles
who cannot escape.

His legs are being digested.
The snake cannot swallow.
The frog cannot escape.
There is only this lesson
I must learn.

You squat beside me
in the mouth of the gorge
and ask me to kill the snake.
I cannot.
It is as if my hands
were wrapped around the sun
and the burning a single note
sung madly in the shelter
of stones and water.

I cannot leave you here
and I cannot go away.

THE SUN HAS BEGUN TO EAT THE MOUNTAIN

Pines eat mist out of the sky
in the village the old
man with yellow eyes
lies stretched out on the mat
he is dying

Stones change shape as they breathe
in the bush the shaman
scrapes the green bark
from the devil's club
she will purge death
again this spring

Birds are silent as day ends
in my silence
I wonder again at the far cities
tell me again
the story of the beginning

You who are near enough to death
please tell me
where the beginning is
look
the sky weeps
the woman comes

Tell me where the sun goes
when the mountains are all eaten
and the world is only a flatness
where eagles fly
cutting the sky to ribbons
with their great wings

THE BLACK FILLY

All day light stuttered
as the slow uncertain hills
were captured by dark clouds
rolling out of the Monashee.
It was when the sky split
that the filly screamed
eyes rolling
tail stretched stiff in the wind.

He smelled it coming.
The charred air and her sweat.
Early in the day he tethered her,
drove a peg in deep, leaving her
earth-bound in the pasture.
When the storm struck she braced
and screamed
heaved at the leather rope.

Between them now is a madness.

Today with mountains firm
under a silent sky he approached her
with soft singing and sweet oats
but she ran to her tethers end
driving to break the binding.

But the peg he buried is deep.

Soon enough she'll come
choking with hunger, weak,
the madness gone with the god
who came to her in her last wildness.

THE BIRD

The bird you captured is dead.
I told you it would die
but you would not learn
from my telling. You wanted
to cage a bird in your hands
and learn to fly.

Listen again.
You must not handle birds.
They cannot fly through your fingers.
You are not a nest
and a feather is
not made of blood and bone.

Only words
can fly for you like birds
on the wall of the sun.
A bird is a poem
that talks of the end of cages.

THE DOG

The dog can no longer
puke up the bones.
He has impaled his guts on greed
and now lies heavy in the weeds
bleeding from his ass.

He has fed on a flying thing
and the bones are cutting him inside.

There is room only
for the crawling things
of the earth to clean
his blood from the grass.

Go now
you who would weep at his dying.

His greed has made him feed
on a flying thing
and he cannot puke up the bones.

MOUNTAIN OYSTERS

Kneeling in the sheep-shit
he picked up the biggest of the new rams
brushed the tail aside
slit the bag
tucked the knackers in his mouth
and clipped the cords off clean

the ram   stiff
with a single wild scream

as the tar went on
and he spit the balls in a bowl.

That's how we used to do it
when I was a boy.

It's no more gawdam painful
than any other way
and you can't have rams fighting
slamming it up every nanny

and enjoyed them with him
cutting delicately
into the deep-fried testicles.

Mountain oysters make you strong

he said
while out in the field

GREY JOHN

Grey John
When your time is up
who will tell you
she is gone?

Everyone said Grey John was good with animals
yet he went to jail for fucking his horse
behind the barn and there was no one
to tell him he wasn't alone

three small boys hiding in the hay
entranced as he balanced on two sawhorses
crooning, stroking her flanks.

Everyone said Grey John was a good man.
He minded his own and now he's in Riverview.
I haven't seen him for a year now
but I saw her today dragging in great circles

a plow over the spring ground
while her new master's whip hovered above her
her flanks shuddering.

She asks me what time it is
as the last truck turns on the brink
of the rotting wall
and bleeds into the fire.
I tell her I don't know.

THE DUMP

In the orange light of burning oil
a woman moves through the wreckage
of cars and broken toilets
face flushed and the urge of wasps
feasting in the light of the sun.
With hands like splintered struts
of fragile doors she cups
her flowered dress
for the gathering of apples.

With a loop of twisted wire
her child flays the decayed head of a coyote.
Flies stitch the air between his feet
with a black crooning to the scattered
maggots. She bends, her belly full of fruit,
and ties the child to her waist
with a twist of binder twine.

OCTOBER

All day I worked in the field
bagging potatoes and turnips,
gathering the last gourds
from among the curled black vines.
All the wandering and women,
the strange roads and stranger times
have led to this: a handful of earth,
a boot on the brittle corn.

I look up at the apples
in the branches I couldn't reach.
Already they have withered.
Soon the storms will come.
Hard from the north
they will strip the trees of leaves.
Like dry brown fists on pillows
the apples will fall into the snow.

THE INTERIOR

It was the feeling he must have had
when he dragged his screaming daughter
from her crib
held her by the heels
and smashed her head against the wall

to kill her
dead like that

The silence he must have felt
when he dropped her on the floor

And that was the Interior
where for days
every father was kind to his child
and when I met them
walking down the street
their children's mouths full of candy

how they smiled
and talked too fast
and couldn't meet my eyes

BUNKHOUSE NORTH

He played with his rifle
as if it was a woman
shot the oiled bolt back and forth
with a neat
　　　　click/snap

and spent his sunday hours
aiming it at everything that moved
until the rest of us in the bunkhouse
twitched each time he softly murmured

pow

each of us remembered
deaths we had delivered:
the gutshot deer
the stumbling bear
snapping at his leg to eat his pain
the falling men pitching on the plain

Each of us wishing he was blooded
or was wise in the loneliness
that comes across the eyes
in that cold quick moment
just after making love

PASSING INTO STORM

Know him for a white man.
He walks sideways into wind
allowing the left of him

to forget what the right
knows as cold. His ears
turn into death what

his eyes can't see. All day
he walks away from the sun
passing into storm. Do not

mistake him for the howl you hear
or the track you think you
follow. Finding a white man

in snow is to look for the dead.
He has been burned by the wind.
He has left too much

flesh on winter's white metal
to leave his colour as a sign.
Cold white. Cold flesh. He leans

into wind sideways; kills without
mercy anything to the left of him
coming like madness in the snow.

THIRTY BELOW

Men on the pond
push logs through constant ice.
Faces stubble with frost.
No one moves beyond the ritual
of work. Torment of metal
and the scream of saws.

Everything is hard. The sky
scrapes the earth at thirty below
and living things pull into pain
like grotesque children
thrown in the wrong season.

Someone curses.
Pulls his hand from the chain.
His skin has been left on steel,
blood frozen into balls.
He is replaced and the work goes on.

Everything is hard.
Cold lances the slow dance
on the pond. The new man trembles
out of control.
He can't hold his pole.
Someone laughs,
says it will be breakup
before they shut this damn mill down.

AFTER

For Pat Lowther

After the machine on the gypo show
caught his arm in its mouth
and chewed the nerves dead
from elbow to finger-tips
he sat in the bar
telling stories for drinks

His best the one about
how he'd lost the use of his arm
changing it every other day
until he ran out of variations
and no one would listen to him
the arm getting in his way
bumping into things
and hanging useless

until the only way
he had of getting a drink
was to lay the dead piece of meat
across the table
and stick pins in it
saying:

It doesn't hurt at all

men laughing
and buying him a drink
for every pin he could hammer in

with his empty glass

FOR RIEL IN THAT GAWDAM PRISON

When Dumont rode with his army
there were only muttered words
of praise at the end; the possible
Messiah praying in his prison . . .

    and how he danced in the circus
    waiting for the clowns to dismount
    while hucksters sold his legend
    to the nickel and dime seats.

There on the prairie there were people
waiting to stop moving. Somewhere
west was too far
and the day eased away into language . . .

    Indians stumbling over buffalo
    in the ring of Madison Square Gardens,
    Gabriel Dumont riding to the dead
    God somewhere over Regina.

SLEEP IS THE SILENCE DARKNESS TAKES

For my father

For breaking forty acres to the plow
pouring my blood into the sun
pulling stone knuckles from the earth
and walking bowed behind a spavined horse
out of the frost of a dead season
following a stoneboat through my thirteenth year
for a share in a crop that was denied
by a father who wouldn't pay a son
for a man's work done

Sleep is the silence darkness takes

Turner Valley was where I starved for youth
until a lady crusted in her trade
lifted me out of a pit of boards and sod
to work in a house of bedrooms where she made
life contain the laughter of the riggers
in a world on the wrong side of the sun
who taught me what it was to be a man
earning the bonus of a year's hard work
in the arms of wild Elsie

Sleep is the silence darkness takes

I broke my body in the hard-rock mines
of depression mountains sucking silica dust
into my swollen lungs until they felt
like bags of blood and glass
but the mountains gave me love
and three small sons until the war
when in the fever of the going
I left them all behind to walk alone
through the graceless falling of my friends
for a dream I did not understand

Sleep is the silence darkness takes

Then the hard days of the returning mind —
the body of my friend still frozen
hanging above the turret of his tank
framed in the flame of the guns
where he remained through the nights
of sweat and jerking dreams —
to a woman who was a stranger with three boys
until I learned that love was bred in pain
and through creation began it all again

struggling through the bitter post-war years
of two more children and three to rediscover
knowing that what was lost
could not be found again

Sleep is the silence darkness takes

And then to be a man and pour my soul
into the pocketbooks of others who stole
my brains and used them for their gain
because of privilege, birth or prior right —
the smiling bastard sons who stayed behind
and built the glass-walled galleys
where I slaved . . . no, not for nothing
but why in the last years I should lie
with a bullet in my heart
when I had come so far, so hard,
to rest here bleeding on a floor and die
and not to know my killer — why?

Sleep is the silence darkness takes

FIVE YEARS

The pine in the corner of the garden
does not lose its needles
nor my tongue its bitter words.
If I am late do not question me.
Five years I have wandered
and on the wind I hear
only the sound of your hands
tearing the dead grass.

In the bar of a city
I drink to the taste of your name
and hear your hands.

The old sun will be reborn
one hundred days before spring comes again
and in the garden where you kneel
pushing the border of the year away
I cry like a cold green king
covering the grass of another season
with the white of winter's cold
before I can come,
if I can come again.

WE TALK OF WOMEN

Sitting in the cookhouse
in the long last hours before sleep
I trade drinks of scotch for tea
with the chinese cook.
His skin is the texture of ricepaper
and his eyes, narrow and black
as crow's wings against the sun,
move below fine wisps of grey
that float on his forehead
like moss on a yellow pine.

We talk of women
in the cold distance of a winter
that has locked us for weeks
inside barriers of snow.

I tell him of a girl at the coast:

>   *All I can remember*
>   *is her hands. When they touched me*
>   *they struggled like captive birds.*
>   *Three months and her face*
>   *is the suggestion of light*
>   *in the window beyond us, eyes*
>   *cold as the barbs of stars*
>   *strung on the wire of night.*

He nods and sits on the low
mattress by the wall.

Over warm wine heated on a candle
we quietly talk:

> *If I could tell you*
> *what she is, I would say*
> *she is made of leaves*
> *and her touch is the sound*
> *of the breath I take*
> *when I climb a mountain.*

> *Yes, I said,*
> *but her memory is winter.*

Moving like a piece of alabaster
born in stone he motions me.
I follow him into his room.
Lighting a candle he leads me
through a dance of startled moths
to the wall beside his bed
where drawings of a woman
delicate as dry wings
hang against the splintered red
of cedar:

> *This is my woman.*
> *She is as young as wind*
> *that rises to melt snow*
> *in the wrong season.*

THINKING ON THAT CONTEST

Thinking on that contest women do
with clothespins in the country
having to hold all the pins in one hand
and they could do it
with hands trained by diapers
and blue workshirts in winter
hand-soaping in a steel tub

as if it was a measure of survival
like an axe falling in a far valley
where sound comes late to you
or not at all
they having learned it in harder times
cursing the cold
clothes hanging frozen to the line
for days going on days
bringing them in piecemeal
to hang over the fire
and let them melt there
reassuming the shape of a man
in time for him to shrug into
before going down to the graveyard
shift at the mines

thinking on that time of trouble
turned into a game
how struggle roots itself in ritual
hands full of clothespins
leaning into wind
never dropping a pin into the snow below

THIRTY MILES IN FROM THE COAST

In the high valleys when the sun dies
a man waits out the death
of his season in silence
carving dreams into masks of fire
in the light from an oil-drum stove.
Winter is measured by the mind—
words that fell from a woman
in another time.

. . . and when she died in the days of snow
choked roads and fallen lines
I rolled her in a canvas
and stored her in the shed until spring.
Thirty miles in from the coast is up
and frost goes down six feet.
It's too hard to dig.

Winter is silence
when ice gathers on crows wings
and nothing can be salvaged from dreams.
In times like these I unwrap her again
to stand in the corner of my mind
like a piece of snow-pounded pine.
Her words are trees that in my mind explode
and cast their fragments
frozen onto the belly of the snow.

TEACHERS

Only a circle of light marks the passing
of the moon in the rising storm. My shadow is
lost in sand as I empty the last scotch.
All day I wrote poems.
Friends and lovers have turned into their lives
like leaves in water turn
slowly to the quiet pools.
Nothing explains this solitude.
What do I want?
Tonight I could load my pack
and wander into the mountains.
By tomorrow I could be
above the clouds watching eagles fly . . .
but I am still here, still
writing poems. Better to buy a bottle
of Teachers Highland Cream
and get drunk with the moon
as it drowns in the sea.

WHITE MOUNTAIN

Trees in glass robes
cold under the moon's cowl.
Arms hold ice.

Wind carries only the howl
of a dog. Ashes of snow
in grey fire.

There is only a faint glow.
Roads of men advance
and retreat.

Tracks fill with snow.

GERALD

He fell in his mother's garden
from the tree where he caught the crow
and when his father found him
he lied
hiding the bird in his coat
and was dragged home
arms crossed upon his chest
to keep the bird alive

was beaten because he cried
and wouldn't thank his god he was alive
and two days later his father
mad at the pride
made him kneel on dried peas
singing hymns into his hands

(how it felt to have nails in his knees
how they danced like liquid fire
telling of withered nights
when he refused to read the bible
and was shipped in his bedroom
with strands of barbed black wire
telling of pain he lived with
laughed at)

But when his father tore off
the head of his pet crow
because he missed church to play
and made him pray
while the headless bird
flopped on the floor

he made a bomb from a coleman stove
and blew his mother's arms off
laughing his way to the garden
flapping his arms
the living sunburst air
full of his despair

while his father knelt in the sacristy
and called on Christ
to curse his wilfulness forever

UNBORN THINGS

After the dog drowns in the arroyo
and the old people stumble into the jungle
muttering imprecations at the birds
and the child draws circles in the dust
for bits of glass to occupy
like eyes staring out of earth
and the woman lies on her hammock
dreaming of the lover who will save her
from the need to make bread again
I will go into the field
and be buried with the corn.

Folding my hands on my chest
I will see the shadow of myself; the same
who watched a father when he moved
with hands on the dark side of a candle
create the birds and beasts of dreams.

One with unborn things
I will open my body to the earth
and watch worms reach like pink roots
as I turn slowly tongue to stone
and speak of the beginning of seeds
as they struggle in the earth;
pale things moving toward the sun
that feel the feet of men above,
the tread of their marching
thudding into my earth.

MACCHU PICCHU

For Earle Birney

I

THE HITCHING POST OF THE SUN

Father Condor, take me,
Brother Falcon, take me,
Tell my little mother I am coming,
For five days I have not eaten or drunk a drop,
Father Messenger, bearer of signs, swift messenger,
Carry me off, I beg you: little mouth, little heart,
Tell my little father and little mother, I beg you, that
I am coming.
> *Death song of condemned lovers.*
> *From the Quechua.*

***

Standing on the highest rung of the city
We place our hands on polished stone
That was a hitching-post for the sun.
Now there is nothing but silence.
We watch the sun fall into the Andes.

The first cold shafts of night
Reach into the river far below.
In a gathering mist I feel
We are growing out of
The body of something dead.

***

Today we lay in the Temple of Virgins
As centuries filled our mouths with moss.
They have stripped away the jungle.
They have torn the winding cloths.
They have scattered bones to the wind.

Strangers walk through the ruins.
They talk of where they come from,
Where they are going.
As we lay in this roofless room
They stoned a snake.

It crawled out of the earth
to lie in the brilliant sun.
Coils of its body like plaited hair,
Eyes of cracked stone. They left it
Broken, draped on a fallen wall.

***

We have been cursed with dreams.
This city was meant to be lost.
Those who died here did not want it found.
I pick up our blanket and find a place
to sleep in the Temple of the Sun.

But even he has hidden his face . . .
Yellow bruise of light, lost to us
Who could heal everything.
We began when the sun fell.
Now there is nothing but shadow.

I imagine women moving with their men.
They surround us with eyes
Here in the high Andes
In a city lost and found again
By men who came to unhitch the sun.

II

THE VIRGINS OF THE SUN

In the jungle tombs they found only women.
One held a child in her womb, hands
Brown roots wrapped around his face.
There were no men.
The city belonged to the Virgins of the Sun.
One by one the tombs were broken,
the Jungle torn away:

> Manco Capac
> And his Incas dead.
> The empire fallen.

> Here they tied the sun at the end of seasons.
> Here they tilled the soil beneath the eyes
> Of warriors who stood between the portals

> Of the sun waiting for the Spanish horse.
> Here the Virgins were buried.
> The Spanish never came.

> Betrayed, the last Inca left for Cuzco
> To bargain with the Viceroy of Spain.
> He died in an ambuscade.

The bridges were cut behind him.
The road forgotten, the jungle grew a mantle
For the dead. The Sun rose and fell on the temple

And in the dark tombs the Virgins slept
Waiting for the Inca to return
And restore them to the Sun.

Let the grave-robbers go.
Let the city grow back to jungle.
Back to the speechless things.
The Virgins have left their tombs
With hands like brown roots,
With their unborn child.
Let the city grow back to jungle.
Let the graves like wounds be closed again.

III

MANCO CAPAC – LAST INCA

Today I leave for the great Capital.
Much has been said of the wisdom
Of this move. In Macchu Picchu
I have ruled. It is as if the empire was

Still water curled in a jug's curve
Spilled like this river into jungle.
Lately numerous stars have crossed
The heaven. As it was for Huaina Capac

So for me. Huarascar and Atahualpa dead.
They have raised the bloodstone cross
In Cuzco. The people are afraid.
But the Viceroy of Spain has asked me

To return. He wishes me in the Temple.
What is that to me? My people burn
In the great square. My houses are
Plundered. The empire come and gone.

The golden rod that was planted in
The beginning is removed . . . melted
For the Three-In-One in Spain.
My warriors will stand at the bridges

And along the great road. If I do not
Return, all will be destroyed.
My people starve in the high passes.
My people die in the streets.

My priests have read the omens.
Still I must go. Perhaps this Spaniard
Speaks truth. I no longer know what
Their truth is. I have spoken to the dead

By the hitching-post of the Sun.
I have returned them to their tombs.
I am Manco Capac, Lord of the Inca.
The words of Pachacutec are my words:

Born like a lily in the garden
I grew like a lily
And when the time came
I withered and died.

THE HUSTLER

In a rainbow bus we begin to descend
a gorge that gapes open like a wound.
The women, who chattered like black beans
in a dry gourd, cover their faces and moan
while the men, not wanting to admit the fear
that turns their knuckles white,
light cigarettes and squint their eyes.

The air fills with hands making crosses.
I make the sign of the cross
with a small grey woman
but she doesn't see me. She has no time
for a gringo when the manifold sins
of a lifetime must be confessed.
Her eyes are buried in the hole
three thousand feet below.

The driver stops the bus, adjusts
the plastic Jesus that obscures
half of his windshield and his eyes—
gets out and stands beside each tire
shaking his head. His face is a scowl
of despair. He kicks each tire in turn,
opens the hood and pounds the carburetor
then gets back on the bus
and crosses himself slowly as the women
begin to weep and children scream.

He mutters two *Pater Nosters*
and a dozen *Ave Marias* as he walks
through the bus with hat extended
to the people who fill it with coins.
He smiles then, bravely, as if the world
had been lifted from his shoulders
and like the thief that Christ forgave
walks out the broken doors to a roadside shrine
and empties his hat into the hands of a Mary
whose expresssion of humility
hasn't changed in a hundred years.

The people sigh and consign their souls to God
and I relax because I saw him as he knelt there
cross his hands on his crotch as if
he were imploring the Mother of God's help
in preserving his manhood on the road to Hell
and pour the collected sucres in his pocket
the price of safety embodied in the vulture
who lifted off her beatific head,
the men shushing their children grandly
and me, peeling a banana and eating,
gazing into the endless abyss.

ELECTION DAY

Sitting in the Language Institute
I listen to a German tell us of the time
he spent four months in the prison
high above the city. Yucca soup and rats
wet walls and the empty eyes of men
who spend lost lives outside the sun.
Two thousand marks from home had given him
his freedom. In the distance the spastic rattle
of machine guns splatter the night.

For three days we have been locked inside
these rooms looking out over Medellin.
The election has been called
and thousands of students have marched
into the city demanding their rights.
Two nuns, a nurse and a boy without legs
ask me to teach them English. The German
laughs. What good is language going to be?
It takes money to go to America.

Kennedy grins beside the passion
of Christ and his hopeless Mother.
Yucca soup and rats, that's all you'll
live for, he says. The boy with no legs
tells me of his uncle who lives in Miami.
Everything is beautiful there, he says.
The radio squawks out the platitudes
of El Presidente. I begin to teach him
my language: the word *knife,* the word *kill.*

CHILE

The girl in the red dress crying
in a small room in a city
the Spanish Conquistadores built
too many years ago to tell
how they poured the lives
of this sad country
into great grey galleons
for shipment back to the court
where a King and Queen
argued about the edge of the world
and a failed fleet somewhere
north in the throat of a sea
they wished they could forget

bends her small brown face
over the photograph
of a brother who was shot
by the carabineros yesterday
and wants an answer I can't give
except to tell the fat American
kid who has been filling her
with acid and disease for weeks
that if he opens his mouth
again to tell me he has learned
to love everyone
I'll fill it with my fist.

THE MAN

Drinking bad whiskey in a bar
on the baked coast of a desert
where the wind never stops moving
and the sand never stops moving
and the sweat never stops moving
down his arms, he wonders
what he is doing beside this woman
whose language he can't speak
and whose body he doesn't know
any better than he knows himself.

He doesn't remember where
he met her or why he is still
with her. He has been watching
two vultures fight over the body
of a rat and he has made a bet
with the fat man who owns the bar
that the bird with one leg will win.

It is the last of his money.
He knows she will leave him
if he loses and he is wondering
what he will do with her if he wins.

THE WOMAN

On a small red stool in a bar
on the baked coast of a desert
where the surf and the sand
and the men have always moved
like years inside her mind
she watches the stranger watching
two vultures fight over the body
of a rat. His skin is so white
and all the hardness that was in him
has drained away like wax off a candle.
It isn't him she wants.

He laughs when the bird
with one leg falls over.
She knows he will leave her.
And it isn't the money.

Hijo de puta.

He smiles. God, she says, God.
He cannot even speak my language,
doesn't know what it is I am
saying, trying not to say, and not.

HER

He sits beside her
and his face is missing
as if someone had taken a knife
and scraped it bare
leaving only the holes
through which he had known her.
It is not love that's left him
bereft of sense. It is not even
that he remembers what she was
before she was gone but that
he must sit there with his hands
buried in the black hair of her
and know that what he has
will never go again.

THE CHILDREN OF BOGOTA

The first thing to understand, Manuel says,
is that they're not children. Don't start feeling
sorry for them. There are five thousand
roaming the streets of this city

and just because they look innocent
doesn't make them human. Any one
would kill you for the price of a meal.
Children? See those two in the gutter

behind that stall? I saw them put out
the eyes of a dog with thorns because
it barked at them. Tomorrow it could be you.
No one knows where they come from

but you can be sure they're not going.
In five years they'll be men and tired of killing
dogs. And when that happens you'll be the first
to cheer when the carabineros shoot them down.

PISSARO'S TOMB

On broad hills, the broken backs of mountains
and the cracks where earth has split from earth
high walls and viaducts, canals and temples
stand rooted in grey stone. But do not speak.
Only the living eye breeds language
where no language is. The words conjured
are only images. The memory of something
in the race that is unknown.

Pissaro stood by these walls
who now lies dried and shrunken
in his tomb beside the sea.
The great cathedral shelters him
where priests walk hooded
beside God. And Pissaro died
who broke an empire into dust.
So it is told in our histories.
And so it was. But the dead do not speak.
Only the living eye breeds language
out of dust. It is what holds this empire
still. This lust for history.

On broken hills the monolithic stones
that once were mountains stand.
Men move upon the land. Pissaro
lies in the capital he built.
The men who were his enemies are gone,
their history unknown, their language lost
as ancient times are lost
though they come and go in me
and will until what now I speak
men know as silence.

THE CAICUSCA

The legend says three thousand men
died for this stone in the mountains.
Fifteen leagues were traversed to this field
in front of the heaving walls of Sacsahuaman
where it lies. It is called *the weary stone.*

Two holes for eyes are drilled into the corner.
From these the legend says it wept man's blood.
The people say the blood came from the stone.
But twenty thousand men who hauled it here
are dead and the fortress says nothing,
ruined, sprawled in the sun.
The stone was for the wall,
the wall was for the men,
the men where for nothing:
what are walls but boundaries for death
that man creates to hide himself behind.
Three thousand men were crushed beneath
a stone that now sits quiet in a field.
The will of man is equal to his walls.

It is the myth of his suffering.
The weight that he carried.
It is called *the weary stone*
but names are made by man for men
as walls are made from mountains in his mind.

FARMERS

Rain falls, the rain has fallen
and will fall again tomorrow.
The slow perceptible sorrow
of the hours and the clamorous
insistence of the rain.
Below black lines of stone
where bits of earth have clung
like flesh to bone the peasants
break this land to seed.

What took a thousand years to be
turns broken into inch-deep graves.
Here only condors live.
The seed goes down and grows
in the ripped skin a harvest
of potatoes like small marbles.
Each plot of land a handful
and no more. It will take
another thousand years to grow
a crop so pitiful again.

Ancient fields are crusted
on the mountains and the men
move on to plant again. No one
attempts to own this land.
The rich control the valleys
and the poor are left with this:
the slow perceptible sorrow
of the rain, the earth and the bodies
of earth's children on the Andes
scraping their lives from stone.

THE CUZCO LEPER

In the morning madness of lost languages
the blind leper sits and sings of night.
The grey bones of his eyes roll
as rosaries of flies like stuttering nuns
circle the remnants of his fingers.
He thrusts his empty bowl
at the sound of the market knives.

He has sat through the morning
and received nothing. The alms he exacts
from the people no longer come.
The fear of his falling apart has been
explained by the doctors from America
and he is no longer considered holy.

A woman, dressed in crusted skirts,
crawls from beneath a cutting table
and fills his bowl with blood.
He drinks
as the flayed and bloody animal
heads stare at him
great mouths empty of tongues.

AT THE EDGE OF THE JUNGLE

At the edge of the jungle
I watch a dog bury his head
in the mud of the Amazon
to drive away the hovering
mass of flies around his eyes.
The swarm expands like a lung
and settles again on the wound.

I turn to where orchids gape
like the vulvas of hanged women.
Everything is a madness:
a broken melon bleeds a pestilence
of bees; a woman squats and pees
balancing perfectly her basket
of meat; a gelding falls to its knees
under the goad of its driver.

Images catch at my skull like thorns.
I no longer believe
the sight I have been given
and live inside the eyes of a rooster
who walks around a pile of broken bones.
Children have cut away his beak
and with a string have staked him
where he sees but cannot eat.

Diseased clouds bloom in the sky.
They throw down roots of fire.
The bird drags sound from its skin.
I am grown older than I imagined:
the garden I dreamed does not exist
and compassion is only the beginning
of suffering. Everything deceives.

A man could walk into this jungle
and lying down be lost
among the green sucking of trees.
What reality there is resides
in the child who holds the string
and does not see
the bird as it beats its blunt head
again and again into the earth.

IT IS SAID

It is said that the butterfly is the soul
of a man just dead and a black cat is holy
when you walk the left-hand path

It is said when you cross the ice
you can see the season's skull dream sleeping fish
who breathe in the current your shadow below

It is said when you warm yourself with burning
you should face an open door
for inside your fire a bird is waiting to be born

It is also said a man does not fear what he is
he fears what he cannot be
but of that knowing no man knows

STILL HUNTING

A single banner of sky between two mountains:
neither the beginning nor the end of clouds.
Somewhere all the animals have happened
and I wait and pray I will know
the difference between the animal and man;
pray for the gift of a death
to break this glacial waste of time—
that when I shoulder the empty body
I will have something to walk with
be it ice, air, stone or man; pray
I will find the road where I left it
in the tree-line far below.

A BEAUTIFUL WOMAN

Mountains, like drifters, never arrive.
Women, like wounds, are what you must survive.
And stones, though they resemble bones,
cannot hold flesh. A beautiful woman
is what you know before you speak it.
The shade your skull casts on your brain.
The space in a stone before you break it.

FROM THE HOT HILLS

For Jaswant Singh Gill

Brought from the hot hills of India
to the cold bleak country of the north
dark men strain bodies into silence
bending and breaking long brown muscles
on the dead weight of timber. Soft
language lost in ignorance
they take the jobs on the green-chain
where no man will work. A job
reserved for drunks who stagger off the train
or the huge bodies of Saskatchewan farm boys
the Sikhs whose names no one knows or cares
to know, respond to *Hey You!* and smile.
Isolate in breathing shacks of snow
they curl their bodies on straw
around the pale flower of a stove
made from a forty-five gallon drum
and fed with salvaged slabs.

In a town of men the women
are alabaster objects
and any Sikh who dares to speak to one
feels the steel toe of a boot.
The biggest joke of winter was the knowledge
they wiped themselves with their fingers
and one day received cheques
wrapped in toilet paper. Stabbed by cold
they breathe pneumonia and the numb
distance of their skin.

Together they wait through the winter
knowing it will take three more
before they can bring their women
from the other side of the world. Locked
into the prison of skin they break
on the long weekend when the loggers
pelt their shack with stones. Three
are taken to hospital in Kamloops
with arms and bellies slashed
and when the lone policeman asks
what caused the fight, they tell him
the fight was amongst themselves.
They say they fought over the memory
of their women; that to keep
from going mad they had driven themselves
there with words, believing they could survive
by telling each other stories of love.

AS IT IS WITH BIRDS AND BULLS

For Margaret Atwood

Having left their women in the dust
outside the sanctuary of the pit
the men, gambling on the blood-line
of birds, hunch with their cocks.
Legs plucked carefully and spiked with spurs
the roosters, born to killing,
beat the still air with wings
and tear at the gloves that bind them.

The sand is cleaned of blood.
Pit-masters rub pepper
under the arched green of tails.
The birds are thrown.

I gamble on the smaller bird
not because he is a coward
but because he seems afraid.
Survival lies in the death you make
believe. As it is with birds and bulls
so with men. They do not hate what they are
they hate what they cannot be.

The survivor crows and falls
blood splurting from his bill.
I collect my money
as the sun stumbles over the line of adobe.
The men sit inside and talk of birds.
The women sit outside and talk of men:
mouths full of coca leaf, they squat
beside gaping bags that receive the dead,
quick fingers tearing
the last feathers from the birds.

THE CARPENTER

The gentle fears he tells me of being
afraid to climb back down each day
from the top of the unfinished building.
He says: I'm getting old
and wish each morning when I arrive
I could beat into shape
a scaffold to take me higher
but the wood I'd need
is still growing on the hills
the nails raw red with rust
still changing shape in bluffs
somewhere north of my mind.

I've hung over this city like a bird
and seen it change from shacks to towers.
It's not that I'm afraid
but sometimes when I'm alone up here
and know I can't get higher
I think I'll just walk off the edge
and either fall or fly

and then he laughs
so that his plum-bob goes awry
and single strokes the spikes into the joists
pushing the floor another level higher
like a hawk who every year adds levels to his nest
until he's risen above the tree he builds on
and alone lifts off into the wind
beating his wings like nails into the sky.

SLASH-BURNING ON SILVER STAR

For John Waterer

The brutal anger that cannot be relieved
except on things. The stump torn from earth
rolls with hanging clots of dirt
into the fire. My hands rage at the roots.
Fear lies in my own defeat
because I do not dare to leave this place;
the elaborate care I take
in pouring diesel on the limbs,
the pride that takes its pleasure
in the flame, the anger
when the packed wet earth won't burn
and the shaking,
the terrible shaking
when its time to quit.

WHAT LITTLE IS LEFT

What little is left is the darkness
under the leaves: the earth
and the geese on the skyline
riding cold wind.
Wingbeat and cry.

We lie and listen to the falling
of leaves. The yellow plunge of
softness breaking silence.

What little is left
pulls into itself and sleeps
with its burden: a leaf
and above its fall
the call of wild geese
as they drift through our darkness
riding the season south.

OBEDIENCE

I learn obedience, Bill,
the perpetual serenity of snow.

There is a benign epitaph in things,
the purgatory of stones in ice.

What have I done that I must praise
this ecstasy? Solitude sits within

me like a mountain, profound,
alien as a wish. Truly I have grieved

for your back in the storm,
grieved at the silence in words. Always

we shall see each other later,
you with your death in that city

broken by a machine and I
consumed by a terrible patience

as I watch the way ice grows in flowers
on the black and empty windows of the night.

OF LETTERS

I sit in the solitude of letters.
Words do not slow the sun.
The sky is clear in the west.

Clouds have passed over me.
Their spun silk hangs
on the bones of the Monashee.

A magpie drifts across the sun.
His long tail writes too swiftly
for me to interpret. On my desk

a wasp I killed last week
after it stung me. Who
will write its poem?

I move toward my fortieth year.
Letters remain unanswered.
The sun slides into the west

and in the east clouds collapse
draping with crystal
the waiting arms of the trees.

SPRING

For Carol

The womb is not there
broken and bleeding
nor the touch of the hand to air
nor the green grass growing
quick in the fields
like the startled eyes
of children when they die.
The sudden burden of the sun
bears down and breaks
the furrows into dust.
As each man breaks in time
the earth to his will
and dreams of the possible
harvest, so you break,
your pains small scratches
on a mystery.

The tree that clings to stone
drops cones upon a barren ground
yet each year bears the privilege
of ice. The seeds of snow.
And the man who opens earth
returns to earth. Late in the night
with the long wind curling sound
where no sound sings, he groans
and turns into his sleep
as you turn into your bruise of silence
heavy with seed, your fingers
curled in fists around the air.

WHEN

When in the silence of night
the pale blister of the moon
walks soft on snow
asleep I go
where nothing can contain me.
There where only birds have walked
with wings I walk
and have no wish to know

what has deranged me. Empty
in the empty fields
I feel the pallid lash
of light on snow, the splash
of moon that hides in hollows
giving shape to darkness
that having given, goes,
leaving no shape of man

but only a small blue mound
as if some animal unearthed
had tried to find its way
back underground
and blind like light is
blind to shadow
without direction
lost itself in snow.

STIGMATA

For Irving Layton

What if there wasn't a metaphor
and the bodies were only bodies
bones pushed out in awkward fingers?
Waves come to the seawall, fall away,
children bounce mouths against the stones
that man has carved to keep the sea at bay
and women walk with empty wombs
proclaiming freedom to the night.
Through barroom windows rotten with light
eyes of men open and close like fists.

I bend beside a tidal pool and take a crab from the se
His small green life twists helpless in my hand
the living bars of bone and flesh
a cage made by the animal I am.
This thing, the beat, the beat of life
now captured in the darkness of my flesh
struggling with claws as if it could tear its way
through my body back to the sea.
What do I know of the inexorable beauty,
the unrelenting turning of the wheel I am inside me?
Stigmata. I hold a web of blood.

I dream of the scrimshawed teeth of endless whales,
the oceans it took to carve them. Drifting ships
echo in fog the wounds of Leviathin
great grey voices giving cadence to their loss.
The men are gone
who scratched upon white bones their destiny.
Who will speak of the albatross in the shroud of the n
the sailor who sinks forever in the Mindanao Deep?
I open my hand. The life leaps out.

ALBINO PHEASANTS

At the bottom of the field
where thistles throw their seeds
and poplars grow from cotton into trees
in a single season I stand among the weeds.
Fenceposts hold each other up with sagging wire.
Here no man walks except in wasted time.
Men circle me with cattle, cars and wheat.
Machines rot on my margins.
They say the land is wasted when its wild
and offer plows and apple trees to tame
but in the fall when I have driven them away
with their guns and dogs and dreams
I walk alone. While those who'd kill
lie sleeping in soft beds
huddled against the bodies of their wives
I go with speargrass and hooked burrs
and wait upon the ice alone.

Delicate across the mesh of snow
I watch the pale birds come
with beaks the colour of discarded flesh.
White, their feathers are white,
as if they had been born in caves
and only now have risen to the earth
to watch with pink and darting eyes
the slowly moving shadows of the moon.
There is no way to tell men what we do . . .
the dance they make in sleep
withholds its meaning from their dreams.
That which has been nursed in bone
rests easy upon frozen stone
and what is wild is lost behind closed eyes:
albino birds, pale sisters, succubi.

AND SAY OF WHAT YOU SEE IN THE DARK

Now with these words the book of the sky
closes. Darkness cries the news to bats
who fly in alphabets no man can read.
The kildeer quiets on her nest
and rests the wing she lied with
when she drew the man away.
Night is the image of running
water and what runs beneath:
stones who know no wind,
trees who lean above
the broken banks their lives.

Darkness crouches. The sky
closes on the animal: the spider
with one leg poised on hunger,
the black fly concealed in leaves.
My fire creates the night
I am surrounded by. The image
and what runs beneath.
The silence following sound.
That which is bound and that
which is undone. This the bond,
the light and the night beyond.

DAY AFTER DAY THE SUN

Day after day the sun hurts these hills into summer
as green returns to stone in filaments as hard as yellow.
Everywhere the old mortality sings.

Sagebrush breaks the bodies of the small.
Dessicated bits of fur huddle in arroyos
as the land drifts away, melted by the heat.

Down by the drying lake a people curl on sand
having nothing more to do with beauty and desire
than to turn their bodies brown. Images of image

they have forgotten the animal who lived in a hole.
Carrion-eater, digger of roots, worshipper of fear.
They burn as an eagle returns from the long weeks hunt

and tears from the bone the breast of a marmot
killed in the hills above Kalamalka.
Satiate she hunches on a dead tree's crest

while below her as she sleeps, magpies,
thin in the thorn trees, more ancient than hunger,
dance their dance of the sun.

IF

Like that dying woman in Mexico
who fed her family by fucking a burro
on a wooden stage in Tiajuana
you are alone and I am drunk again
on tequila, refusing to die,
hearing the madness of the burro
as the woman wept with pain . . . you are
naked and I no longer want you.
If I could choose a last vision
it would be the dream of the knife,
the dream of the death of pain.
Put on your clothes.
I am obscene.
I am one of those who laughed
when the burro dropped her on the floor.

AT THE EDGE OF THE

At the edge of the
field the fence gathers
leaves of the year.
Two magpies in the acacia.
They fatten on the last dead,
old field mice
and the heads of moles
left by the hunting cats.
The farmer picks by hand
spare stalks of winter wheat.
He has gone over the ground
again and again
nothing is wasted.

THE WITNESSES

To know as the word is known, to know little
or less than little, nothing, to contemplate
the setting sun and sit for hours, the world
turning you into the sun as day begins again

To remember words, to remember nothing
but words and make out of nothing the past,
to remember my father, the McLeod Kid
carrying the beat, riding against time

On the rodeo circuit of fifty years ago
the prairie, stretched wet hide
scraped by a knife, disappearing everywhere
to know the McLeod Kid was defeated

To know these things
to climb into the confusions
which are only words, to climb into desire
to ride in the sun, to ride against time

The McLeod Kid raking his spurs on the mare
the cheers from the wagon-backs
where the people sit to watch the local
boy ride against the riders from Calgary

To spit melon seeds into the dust
to roll cigarettes, to leave them hanging
from the lip, to tip your hat back and grin
to laugh or not laugh, to climb into darkness

Below the stands and touch Erla's breast
to eat corn or melons, to roll cigarettes
to drink beer, bottles hidden in paper bags
to grin at the RCMP, horseless, dust on their boots

To watch or not watch, to surround the spectacle
horses asleep in their harness, tails switching
bees swarming on melon rinds, flys buzzing
and what if my words are their voices

What if I try to capture an ecstasy that is not
mine, what if these are only words saying
this was or this was not, a story told to me
until I now no longer believe it was told to me

The witnesses dead, what if I create a past
that never was, make out of nothing
a history of my people whether in pain
or ecstasy, my father riding in the McLeod Rodeo

The hours before dawn when in the last of darkness
I make out of nothing a man riding against time
and thus my agony, the mare twisted sideways
muscles bunched in knots beneath her hide

Her mane, black hair feathered in the wind
that I believe I see, caked mud in her eyes
the breath broken from her body and the McLeod Kid
in the air, falling, the clock stopped.

EVEN THOUGH SHE HAS BEEN PUSHED

Even though she has been pushed
into the farthest corner

and the call Last Call
has begun to empty the bar

and the half-full glass beside her
is so dead it looks like urine

and the men with her argue
about who won or lost the game

tonight she is beautiful
with her hair in knots

around her sleeping face
and the small red worm of blood

just beginning to cake
below her broken nose

and the fingers of her hand
like a stilled pendulum

not quite grazing a carpet
that once was green

she is still
still beautiful

WILD BIRDS

Because the light has paled and the moon
has wandered west and left the night
to the receding sea we turn into ourselves
and count our solitudes. The change
we might have wished for had we time

to wish is gone. The sacrifice of hours
has endured and we remember nothing of our days.
Neither the hand with the knife nor human gift
is enough to bring fulfillment. Form that was never
ours, the questioning of paradise, the beauty of

our minds. Once beyond the sight of land
I saw a flock of crows battle the wind.
Baffled, returning, knowing the landfall,
they beat their wings against a strength
greater than their own. We are all of us

as those birds I saw at sea blown outward
against our will. I read the books
and dreamed the dream that words could change
the vision, make of man a perfect animal
and so transformed become immortal.

What else was there to dream? Not this,
not this beating against the wind. Chaos
is our creation and the god we wished was man:
to turn again into the thing we are, yet be
black cinders lost at sea, the wild birds failing.

FOR PAT LOWTHER

If mouths are words then poems are
what we die with if we die at all
our bodies bones a syllable can't find
our flesh no more than wind inside a tree

begging leaves the cold has caught
and breathed into a whiteness not our own.
Forget the punctuation marks of crows
the expletive a worm is

when he eats our troubled dying on the road.
We live with what we always knew we were.
A word is not a mouth
and not the moment just before

we thought we'd live. The poem of one just dead
is the opening a mouth made in our flesh
before the flesh could speak, the I
before the I, the unhealed wound of all we ever knew

ICE STORM

As if the snow was more than just a prison.
Ice like an eyelid closing on the birds
beneath the snow. As I am more than just

the owner of this field, knowing every bird
I free, I'll find another dozen dead.
My foot jerks back from cold,

angry now, shaking my fists at the rare
explosions below me, feet breaking through
the icy cloud cover of their tombs.

THE TRACE OF BEING

For Brian Fawcett

Drunk, the poison breathing in my body,
pain, I am no more than the camels
who died here in search of the deserts
they remembered. Think of them wandering
the upland plateau, avoiding the natural
world they were strangers to.

Moose, elk and deer, the cougar's cough
polite before killing, the bear's paw
printed deep in sand beside the sprawling
wrecks of rotting salmon, the trees
stark, bones in snow, and the camels
chimera, ghosts, the last one dead.

Walking the city I read the desires,
obituaries, bitter poems in praise,
memories of the days and nights spent
waiting for desire, for praise.
The beautiful machines. The poems
of desire, of praise, the terrible vanities.

The beautiful women, the uncompromising
men who are their companions, those
who no longer doubt, who are already
ancestors, the pride that worships things,
great monoliths, erected stone, gestures
to the endless vision called property.

I have begun to believe myself.
A tragedy for a poet who wanted to be
a poet. In spite of everything.
In spite. In anger, confusion, pain,
the transfigured, enigmatic, the tears
of ruin, the body wronged from the start.

Why are the McLean Boys in my mind?
Why are they always vicious punks
who murdered out of fear? Why not
heroic like Bill the Kid? Why
was I always them? The dying gods?
Peter's journey to Rome? Fish on stone?

The trace of being, the impossible wreckage
of the human, without respite, without cease,
turning and turning in spite of prophecy,
corrupt, history without holiness, the gone
peoples, the endless rituals, the dead
and those who accompany them, singing.

IN EVERY WORLD

'I hold the law
I keep the mysteries true'   —HD

Grass struggles with the edge of man's desire
for order, here at the base of the concrete
where she lies, her body splayed on stone.
Blood from her broken skull has filled her eyes
and she cannot see but drunkenly smears it
with her palms across her face. Her cry is
the last of the human, a sound
that like a child's is all surrender.

Out of the cracks the green grass lifts in tongues
to speak her clean. She tells them nothing.
Truth is to be glimpsed, no more,
an element as much of life as is a slug's death
on a hill of salt. The hours cover me.

Bats hold the night together
while dogs rage in their season for the bitch
keeping from the suitors jaws their paws.
To be lame is to die in that world.
In every world.
And what is law and what is mystery?
To name her with the living, with the dead?
To take her home?

She has no home.
Ants in pure procession come
to bear away the feast.
Morning brings flies.
I leave her where she lies and drunk
continue with night, its breast of moon, its stars;
how, as I cry, they burst among the clouds
and then are lost in the turning of the wind.

AS I CARE

As I care for the opening in the clouds
and the clouds opening before me
like the eyes of a man in a room
who sees for one moment walls
from a bed he cannot rise from
so I care for the open window
and the cries of the man below.

His body has grown older than he imagines
and in the night he begs it
to lift him from where he lies.
His love will not allow him windows.
The wind parts the clouds
so I care though I know nothing
and nothing can be known.

See where the clouds open, see
where the clouds for one moment open
and the moon, gone down to darkness
so far back in the memory
it is as if it has always been gone
returns, tentative, slow
with that first glow of evening

when light is not light
when eyes are for one moment afraid
and the why of what we are reaches out
to touch whatever it is lying next to us
so long as it be alive
so long as it be something
more than nothing but ourselves.

A MURDER OF CROWS

It is night and somewhere
a tree has fallen across the lines.
There was a time when I would have slept
at the end of the sun and risen with light.
My body knows what I betray.
Even the candle fails, its guttering stub
spitting out the flame. I have struggled
tonight with the poem as never before
wanting to tell you what I know—
what can be said? Words are dark rainbows
without roots, a murder of crows,
a memory of music reduced to guile.
Innocence, old nightmare, drags behind
me like a shadow and today I killed again.

The body hanging down from its tripod.
My knife slid up and steaming ribbons of gut
fell to the ground. I broke the legs
and cut the anus out, stripped off the skin
and chopped the head away; maggots of fat
clinging to the pale red flesh. The death?

If I could tell you the silence
when the body refused to fall
until it seemed the ground reached up
and pulled it down. Then I could tell you
everything: what the grass said
to the crows as they passed over,
the eyes of moss, the histories of stone.

It is night and somewhere
a tree has fallen across the lines.
Everything I love has gone to sleep.
What can be said?
The flesh consumes while in the trees
black birds perch waiting first light.
It is night and mountains
and I cannot tell you what the grass said
to the crows as they passed over
can only say how when I looked
I lost their bodies in the sun.

HOW THE HEART STINKS WITH ITS DEVOTIONS

For the brothers D'Amour and Johnny Gringo

How the heart stinks with its devotions—
Rot my wisdom, I am drowned
In the poisonous storms of the mind.
To remember dying
Buried in the surge of the dance.
Empty your eyes of all save form.
It is the green perfection of the space
A leaf includes in its growing,
The delicate birth baffled by the wind.
Ah, heart, I cannot scorn the armies of your pain.
It is night, air, and I am drunk again on words.
One stone would be enough,
One leaf a feast.